Translation *as* Transhumance

Photograph of the shepherd René Alcazar taken by Patrick Fabre in 2007 in the Gorges du Bachelard, France.

Translation *as* Transhumance

MIREILLE GANSEL
Translated by Ros Schwartz
FOREWORD BY LAUREN ELKIN

FEMINIST PRESS
AT THE CITY UNIVERSITY OF NEW YORK
NEW YORK CITY

Published in 2017 by the Feminist Press
at the City University of New York
The Graduate Center
365 Fifth Avenue, Suite 5406
New York, NY 10016

feministpress.org

First Feminist Press edition 2017

Copyright © 2012 by Éditions Calligrammes
Translation copyright © 2017 by Ros Schwartz
Foreword copyright © 2017 by Lauren Elkin
Traduire comme transhumer was originally published in France by Éditions Calligrammes in 2012.

This work received the French Voices Award for excellence in publication and translation. French Voices is a program created and funded by the French Embassy in the United States and FACE (French American Cultural Exchange). French Voices Logo designed by Serge Bloch.

 This book was made possible thanks to a grant from New York State Council on the Arts with the support of Governor Andrew Cuomo and the New York State Legislature.

Ros Schwartz would like to thank Natasha Lehrer for her sensitive and insightful editing and for her deep commitment to this project.

First printing November 2017

Cover and text design by Drew Stevens

Library of Congress Cataloging-in-Publication Data
Names: Gansel, Mireille, author. | Schwartz, Ros, translator.
Title: Translation as transhumance / Mireille Gansel ; translated by Ros
    Schwartz.
Other titles: Traduction en transhumance. English
Description: New York : The Feminist Press at CUNY, [2017]
Identifiers: LCCN 2017012003 (print) | LCCN 2017038296 (ebook) | ISBN
    9781936932085 (ebook) | ISBN 9781558614444 (softcover)
Subjects: LCSH: Translating and interpreting. | Gansel,
    Mireille--Translations into English. | BISAC: LITERARY COLLECTIONS /
    Essays. | BIOGRAPHY & AUTOBIOGRAPHY / Personal Memoirs. | BIOGRAPHY &
    AUTOBIOGRAPHY / Cultural Heritage. | BIOGRAPHY & AUTOBIOGRAPHY /
    Women.
Classification: LCC P306 (ebook) | LCC P306 .G27413 2017 (print) | DDC
    418/.02--dc23
LC record available at https://lccn.loc.gov/2017012003

Native language is not a set of grammar rules and regulations, it is the child's spiritual nourishment.
—Janusz Korczak

FOREWORD

In this beautiful memoir of a life lived in and through translation, Mireille Gansel defines the process of bringing words from one language to another as a kind of seeking, tied to the land. *Transhumance* refers to the seasonal movement of a shepherd and his flock to another land, or *humus*. It is the opposite of settling and farming: it is a form of nomadism, a search for richer grass, and it provides an apt image for her own trajectory as a translator.

Gansel was drawn to the German spoken by her family, reduced to a "little circle of survivors" after the Holocaust. That Gansel works on German makes her particularly attuned to the movement of and within languages. Just as Adorno said there could be no poetry after Auschwitz, Gansel suggests here that the German language itself is utterly changed after the Shoah. "This is the German that has been punctuated by exiles and passed down through the generations, from country to country, like a violin whose vibratos have retained the accents and intonations, the words and

expressions, of adopted countries and ways of speaking."
Translation as Transhumance is a family history of languages
and exiles, asking: What does a language retain of the vio-
lence it has been used to commit? "How do you bridge the
abyss created in the German language by the barbed-wire
fences and watchtowers of history? How do you reach the
shores of a language of the soul?" The twentieth century is
a bloody field, but how can we move away from it? What
kinds of bloody footprints do we track elsewhere? Memory
and history are the translator's terrains.

There are physical boundaries, too. The Berlin Wall
stands between Brecht and Gansel's rendering of his work;
she is not only a shepherd with a flock but a smuggler,
slipping language past the guards. Foolish are the leaders
who build walls around their countries, thinking they can
keep the desired in and the feared out; doomed to fail are
those who try to police or purify a language. Wherever
totalitarianism or censorship takes hold, it is the role of
the translator to find a way up and over the wall.

The conquering of the Czech lands by the German
language affects Gansel's translations of an East German
poet, Reiner Kunze, whose work she tells us was deeply
influenced by Czech poetry. She describes the prob-
lem of rendering a phrase, *sensibel wege*, in French, first
rendering the *wege*, paths, as "fragile," then, years later,
retranslating them as "sensitive." Just as a piece of writing
can never be finished as long as its writer is alive to revise

it, or as long as scholars are interested in accounting for its drafts and revisions, so a translation can be thought of as provisional, momentary. In his own wonderful book on translating Rilke, William Gass writes that what is produced when the translator has finished his work is "a reading enriched by the process of arriving at it, and therefore, really, only the farewells to a long conversation"; this puts me in mind of Walter Benjamin's description of the work as the "death mask of its conception." For Gansel the farewells are temporary, and the death mask can yawn back to life. "At that moment," Gansel writes, "I understood translation both as risk-taking and as continual re-examination, of even a single word—a delicate seismograph at the heart of time."

We move from Germany to North Vietnam, where Gansel journeyed during the war, "to confront McNamara's declaration that the US would 'bomb 'em back to the stone age' with the testimony of a culture that was several thousand years old." They would publish for the first time in French an anthology of Vietnamese poetry, as an answer to McNamara's threat. In Vietnam, Gansel learned to play the monochord to capture the "cantillation" of Vietnamese poetry, to help her go beyond clever French poetic devices of alliteration and onomatopoeia into "a vast and entirely different kind of poetry"—capturing in French the "wordless voice" of the Vietnamese. She describes her process of moving from a word-for-word translation to a more nuanced framework of meanings and clarifications, to a third stage, in which she would arrange "all the notes, sounds, images, and narratives in such a way as to recreate the words, structures, and rhythms of an entire oral heritage."

And we move, we transhume, again, from North Vietnam to the South of France, where Gansel asks René Char for some of his poems to give to her Vietnamese mentor to translate. On the road away from Char's home, the idea of translation as transhumance occurs to Gansel, who reflects on "the long, slow movement of the flocks to distant places, in search of the greenest pastures, the low plains in winter and the high valleys in summer":

> All the ancient routes that have witnessed encounters and exchanges in all the dialects of the "umbrella language" of Provençal. So it is with the transhumance routes of translation, the slow and patient crossing of countries, all borders eradicated, the movement of huge flocks of words through all the vernaculars of the umbrella language of poetry.

In stringing these encounters together, Gansel helps us understand that translation is more than a grammar; it is a listening. When we translate, we are not rendering a block of text in its immediate equivalent; we keep an ear out for what is unspoken, carried through language, smuggled inside of it. Sometimes this means turning to people who can perceive the echoes in language that we cannot, even in our own native tongues.

Gansel gleaned this while translating the ethnographic writings of Eugenie Goldstern, a refugee in Vienna who was driven by pogroms from Odessa in 1905 only to perish at Sobibór in 1942. Wandering in the Alps, Goldstern produced her work in a space removed from languages and nations, "among the rockrose and the rosemary"; she "recorded the minutiae of day-to-day lives in the villages, hamlets, and alpine pastures on the fringes and the shattered borders of Europe in the first quarter of the twentieth century." Her work prompts Gansel to ask how to render incredibly specific language: what "complementarity" could exist in French to capture a language "that weaves between the remotest places and is composed of all the nuances and preciseness of their idioms, sayings, and names across the Alps, from Slovenia to Savoie, from Piedmont to Tyrol, via the canton of Valais and Les Grisons?" It requires that Gansel defamiliarize her native French.

Languages themselves contain multitudes; they cannot be assimilated or colonized because they are local, personal, and yet—for Gansel—universal, transcendent, resistant. They are composed of a million gestures, movements, exchanges, substitutions; when we speak or write in other languages, we give voice to the essential chiasma at the heart of all our encounters. I am always you; you are always I. *Je est un autre.* Sitting in a house in the high Swiss valley where Goldstern walked and wrote, Gansel suddenly understands this: "as I sat at the ancient table beneath the blackened beams," Gansel recalls, "it suddenly dawned on me that the stranger was not the other, it was me. I was the one who had everything to learn, everything to understand, from the other."

—Lauren Elkin,
Paris, 2017

LISTENING TO THE SILENCES

Whenever a letter arrived from Budapest, Father would become engrossed in reading it. The entire household held its breath and a reverent silence reigned. Sitting there in the big armchair, he was suddenly far away. Then, with ritual solemnity, he would announce: "Tonight, I am going to translate for you." No one ever failed to be there or dared to be late. I recall listening to the silences while Father struggled to find the right word or sentence construction, sometimes stopping short and correcting himself. Mysterious gaps, tenuous bridges. The little girl loved hearing the words that spoke about her, and better still, hearing them uttered by this father who was so sparing with his compliments. One evening in particular stands out in my memory, when for the first time I experienced viscerally, without yet realizing its significance, what "translation" would come to mean for me. It all happened with the utmost simplicity, as is often the case when something is important. To my delight, the section of the letter my father was reading was about me. He initially translated a word used by his brother or one of his sisters as "beloved," stumbled over the next word and repeated this—actually rather ordinary—adjective once, stumbled again, and then repeated it a second time. That triggered something in me. I dared to interrupt him. I asked: "But in Hungarian, is it the same word?" He replied evasively: "It means the same thing!" Undeterred, I pressed him: "But what are the words in Hungarian?" Then, one by one, he enumerated, almost with embarrassment, or at least with a certain reticence, as though there were something immodest about it, the four magic words which I have never forgotten: *drágám, kedvesem, aranyoskám, édesem*. Fascinated, I relentlessly pestered him, begging him to translate for me what each word meant. *Drágám*, my darling; *kedvesem*, my beloved; and two other words whose sensual literalness I would never forget: *aranyoskám*, my little golden girl; *édesem*, my sweet. That evening I discovered that words, like trees, had roots whose magic my father had revealed to me: *arany*, gold; *édes*, sweet; each of these terms enriched by a lovingly enveloping possessive. All of a sudden, the blueprint of my native French glowed from within.

Those four words opened up another world, another language that would one day be born within my own language—and the conviction that no word that speaks of what is human is untranslatable.

"DO YOU KNOW THE LAND . . ."

Father had added a further damper to the *ukase* banning the Hungarian language: "If you wish to communicate with the family, you will simply have to learn German."

"But do *you* know German?" Father's reply was chilling: "I know eight words, the ones the teacher reserved for the Jewish students in the class—the only ones he dinned into me: '*Du bist ein Stück Fleisch mit zwei Augen*' ('You are a piece of meat with two eyes')." Then he said: "I hate German." Many years later, the little girl would understand that in the dark waters of a shared suffering and a shared rebellion, this hatred developed into a dual rejection: of German, the language of the persecutors and those who humiliate, and of Hebrew, the language of his Jewish-self, his persecuted and humiliated self. From his childhood in Balassagyarmat he harbored a lifelong rejection of any doublespeak. Of any betrayal of the Word. Of the language of the Prophets: the Hebrew of his pious mother Deborah, from a long line that

3

came originally from Moravia, and the Hebrew prayers of his father Nathan, from a long line that came from Galicia. Countries on the very margins of the Austro-Hungarian Empire, created at the moment of the partition of Poland in 1772, then wiped from the world map in 1918. The crossroads of the languages spoken by all the peoples it comprised: Polish, Ruthenian, German, Yiddish. Places of wretchedness and violent persecutions where the poorest Jews drew on the mystical roots of an intense piety: Hasidism, *hasid—hesed,* goodness and fervor of the heart. And so it was with Grandfather Nathan, a typesetter in a small printing works, who brought to life the sacred texts in the humble gestures to which the Sabbath gave their full meaning. Every Saturday, dressed in his threadbare but respectable black suit, he would do the rounds of all the hospitals in Budapest on foot, sit at the bedsides of the sick who had no visitors, talk with them, and then take a sweet from his pocket and give it to them. On leaving the synagogue on a Friday evening, he would never let a solitary fellow worshipper go off alone into the night, but always invited him to join his large family around the table.

These memories were recounted to me by my old Aunt Szerenke, in the German of which Aharon Appelfeld once wrote: "It was not the language of the Germans but that of my mother. . . . In her mouth the words had a pure sound, as if she were speaking them inside an exotic bell jar. . . . The words of the languages around us seeped into us without our knowing it. The four languages flowed together into one, rich in nuances, contrasting, satirical, full of humor. In this language, there was a lot of space for feelings, for the subtlety of emotions, for imagination, and for memory."

This is the German of Imre Kertész from Budapest; of Aharon Appelfeld from Czernowicz; of Tibor, the family's last patriarch, from Prague. When I hear their voices, when they speak to me, whether in Berlin, Jerusalem, or Haifa, I hear Aunt Szerenke's voice and that entire little circle of survivors, all speaking the same language, from a world that is no more.

This is the German that has been punctuated by exiles and passed down through the generations, from country to country, like a violin whose vibratos have retained the accents and intonations, the words and expressions, of adopted countries and ways of speaking.

This is the German that has no land or borders. An interior language. If I were to hold on to just one word, it would be *innig*—profound, intense, fervent.

This is the German partly learned at school in the days of the Austro-Hungarian Empire, and partly a cross-border language within the family. This was especially true of Aunt Szerenke, who had not gone to school but who, as the eldest of nine siblings, absorbed the private language of her parents: Nathan, born in Hungary, and Deborah-Charlotte, born in Slovakia. German was the language of their marriage; Hebrew, the language of their prayers. Aunt

Szerenke was a well of memory. She left certain things unspoken, but between the words the silence of her smile expressed the essential, her infinite understanding of people's lives.

As soon as she learned that I had chosen to study German at the *lycée*, she wrote me a letter, on paper like a sheet of sky, as light as a wing. My first letter from "over there" for which I had no need of a translator. Her handwriting danced between the lines, echoing the rhythm of her words that had been composed out loud and were uninterrupted by any punctuation. She nominated me her "secretary": "Even if I don't know how to write them very well, I know you understand the words that are in my heart." The ultimate honor, straight from the heart. I was now authorized to receive and keep secrets, just as the little writing desk received them, as well as to transcribe words from a language that we would always share. I became a secretary; it was my first job and the first step on the different paths that would lead me to translation. This was how I discovered a German that went far beyond the classroom walls and the school curriculum. Was not this language of the soul, which had defied so many prisons, so many frontiers, by its very essence the language of poetry? It resonated with me from the beginning, something that I recognized when, leafing through my textbook, an edition still printed in Gothic script, I first came across a poem in German, some lines by Goethe:

Kennst du das Land, wo die Zitronen blühn,
Im dunkeln Laub die Gold-Orangen glühn

> Do you know the land where the lemon-trees bloom,
> the golden oranges glow amid the dark leaves[1]

I experienced the same enchantment as when, in the leafy shade of the little garden of the house on Mandula Street, Aunt Szerenke, drawing from that age-old well, would tell me endless stories in her idiosyncratic German peppered with Hungarian, Yiddish, and Slovak. The same enchantment as when, on summer nights with my elderly Uncle István, snuggled in blankets under the huge trees of Margaret Island, we listened to Schubert's Lieder ascending to the stars.

LANGUAGE IN EXILE

Just one room, with a high ceiling and those big English bay windows. One room to live in. The home of an exile, Mitzi, Grandmother Deborah's niece, and her elderly mother, Emma, who had been born in Poland. The room was allocated to them by the British refugee office when, right after the *Anschluss*, the government opened the border for one month to Czechoslovakian nationals living in Vienna. In a corner, behind a screen, a wash basin and, just next to it, a two-ring gas cooker. Two narrow divans upholstered in worn velvet, and a sagging armchair and two chairs around a small table. An old suitcase on top of the wardrobe, the toilet along the hall. And the electricity meter, which you have to feed with coins to have light when dusk falls or when the London sky is grey and lowering. London, where, after the war, they were reunited with a cousin, the conductor Rudolf Schwartz—the sole survivor of his large Slovakian family—who was deported to Auschwitz and then, thanks to Furtwangler, released. Only to be sent to Sachsenhausen and Bergen-Belsen.

One summer's day, for the first time, Mitzi broached the past. Past in the present, past so present, with everything it had deposited in this room that suddenly seemed so vast. Everything that the grim tide deposits on the shores of a life. A bit like picking up and reassembling the fragments of a clay vase shattered by history, swallowed up by the Holocaust. Perhaps an attempt to alleviate the absence, so many absences; to hear voices again, their voices.

Whatever the reason, that summer evening I quietly closed the door and paid a visit to the Bodleian Library. Perhaps because every archive in that timeless place is a memorial. At the entrance to the reading room, you hand over your pens and pencils—you are not allowed to make notes in the margins here. A place to read: *lesen*—which also means to gather or glean. In monastic silence, beneath the vaulted Gothic ceiling, I opened the somber chronology and turned one by one the darkest pages of the Nazi atrocities in Slovakia.

Mitzi, with her large eyes the color of night, lively and yet melancholy. A batik artist, she had wanted to enroll at the Vienna School of Arts and Crafts, but she was barred: because of her Czech passport? Or because she was Jewish? In London, she earned her keep making soft toys and lived in that one room, even after her mother's death, until the end of her life. In the little courtyard, she had planted a tiny

fir tree that she had once brought back from the Wiener-
wald she so loved. But she knew there was no place for her
in that Austria where, on each of her rare trips, she felt the
unspeakable, intangible, tightening grip of anti-Semitism.
She spoke in German, for her a highbrow language, as if
those centers of intellectual life as she called them—Brno,
in Moravia, and Prague—where "cultured" Jews gathered,
were still in existence. She said that word, *kultiviert*, with
pride, even reverence. For her, it still had the special aura it
had acquired during the time of Franz Joseph's empire and
had kept intact since the age of Enlightenment, protected
from the political instrumentalization of *Kultur* in Bis-
marck's Germany. One word, the embodiment of dignity
for generations of Central European Jews. And in the hier-
archy of those intellectual values, Mitzi, entirely lost in her
recollections, mixed up tenses and times, abruptly switch-
ing to the present as she tried to bring into focus the inner
images that haunted her, drawing on that cross-border lexical crucible: "*Prag ist ein kolossales geistiges Zentrum—auch
Brünn*" ("Prague is a huge intellectual center, as is Brno").
She added a sentence whose syntactic architecture was
both rigorous and baroque, like the German spoken on the
Viennese banks of the Danube: "*Auch geistig hochstehende
intellektuelle Leute sind nach Wien oder an Budapest gefahren*"
("Intellectual academic highbrows, too, went to Vienna or
to Budapest"). How do you translate the ascending movement of that spiral of adjectives extolling the spiritual and

intellectual superiority of those who left for Vienna and Budapest? An ornately crafted German derived directly from the language of Joseph Roth, Franz Kafka, and Martin Buber, in which she relished telling me in an immutable present tense about the villages of Moravia and the area around Bratislava where members of her vast family had settled. This relative is a sheep farmer on land he was able to acquire when the Jews were emancipated under the Empress Maria Theresa; that one works in an aristocrat's plum brandy distillery; another farms a plot of land rented from a Christian count; several are craftsmen. In the hugely rich and versatile palette of that German, where so many languages intersected, she reveled in finding the subtlest nuances and colors to evoke the Gypsy villages, the sheep in the twilight haze, the beauty of the cornfields, and in the evenings, after sunset, the tray in the kitchen, with milk for the rabbi who came by to give his blessing. A whole world, now lost, with not one trace of a single survivor.

In the semidarkness, Mitzi reminisced quietly. She spoke almost in a whisper. In that language of memory, language of the mind, language without a home. Language in exile.

SALVAGED LANGUAGE

Aunt Renée's eyes look as if they have been hewn from the crystal blue of twilight. This silver-haired elderly lady is one of Grandfather Nathan's nieces. Her voice sounds surprisingly familiar. I close my eyes and I hear Szerenke— the same register, the same intonations. On the table in the little kitchen, the Sabbath candles are lit. The French window is open onto the rose garden that Uncle Eduard lovingly tends in this religious section of one of the oldest kibbutzim in Israel. Recently arrived from Czechoslovakia, during the final days of the Prague Spring, he is putting down new roots by tending his flower beds. Bending over the earth, he weeds, prunes, waters, and contemplates, in infinite silence and with infinite patience. That same silence that echoed around their daughter's table, where I first met them, at her apartment outside Tel Aviv. A gulf of silence between them and their grandson Judah, who is celebrating his twentieth birthday surrounded by his army friends. A gulf of silence, for want of a common language. Not Czech, nor Hungarian, nor German, nor Yiddish. Vectors of an entire world, culture, history, memory. So many internal wellsprings now forgotten, buried beneath the thick layer of the noncommunicated, the noncommunicable.

Sabbath evening in the little blue kitchen, the fine white hand-embroidered tablecloth appears even whiter in the flickering candlelight. Aunt Renée and Uncle Eduard pray in Hebrew and chant the psalms with a gentle, grave joy. Then, in the quiet of the evening, in soft, low, solemn voices, they bring back to life a world that has been swallowed up. So many murdered loved ones, whom they alone remember and commemorate.

Taking turns, sometimes speaking at the same time, they tell their stories as if drinking long drafts from the fount of their lives, as if the starry night will never end. They speak in a German accented with all its neighboring languages: Hungarian, Czech, Yiddish. Language of the soul, language without a home. Salvaged language.

A TREE PLANTED BY THE POET

When I was thirteen or fourteen, I was given a school
travel grant. We wandered through the ruins of Dresden. I
didn't know then that it was the Allies who had deliberately
reduced an area of light and beauty to ashes. An area without borders, belonging to an entire people, to all peoples. I
didn't yet know that there are silences that are also ways of
rewriting history. I saw an old woman begging beside the
Elbe. I began to speak to her, but the teacher accompanying
us came over to stop me. Those gagged words haunted me
for a long time; I felt a sense of betrayal. The words of the
other, words reaching out to the other. Failing to take the
step, to cross the border. I have never forgotten that broken
figure in her black shawl, a German woman in mourning.

In Weimar, Goethe's house on the vast Frauenplan. The
first time I had been inside a poet's home. I walked around
it with reverence, as if it were a sanctuary of the mind. I was
looking for slivers of life, of presence, in that huge mansion
that had remained intact amid so many ruins. An absence

that was peopled by poems. The voice of the poems I had just discovered and which spoke to me as though they were written in a private language. On that trip, I was also taken to Buchenwald. I did not know then that two or three years earlier, there had still been deportees there, prisoners of the Soviet police. In the camp's deserted avenues, we were told about the struggle of the anti-fascists. One of the things I remember from that day is a huge, black death slab made of concrete or cement. A screed of silence. I didn't know yet what I would later discover—that words and silences can be used to create languages known as doublespeak. And one day too I would find out that at Buchenwald there was "somewhere within the area of our camp, so they say, marked with a commemorative plaque and protected from us prisoners by a fence, a now nobly spreading tree, planted with his own hand,"[1] by the poet Goethe. Imre Kertész wrote those words with the eyes and words of his fourteen-year-old self, a Jewish child deported to Buchenwald.

Many years later, in a Berlin café, he told me that although he wrote in Hungarian, he still thought in the German of the Austro-Hungarian Empire. That supranational, cross-border language in which he had grown up. An impregnable territory which no barbed-wire fence, no watchtower, would ever be able to restrict or enclose, over which no barbarism would ever be able to cast its shadow.

THE FRUITS OF THE ELDERBERRY TREE

How do you bridge the abyss created in the German language by the barbed-wire fences and watchtowers of history? How do you reach the shores of a language of the soul?

It was cold and gloomy that night in the small room at the Collège de France. But at somber times in our lives, we occasionally come across brilliant individuals who light up the darkness. An elderly man with an ice-blue gaze entered the room. Robert Minder, an eminent Germanist and unflagging anti-Nazi from the very start of World War II. He was Albert Schweitzer's intellectual and musical companion, his heir and executor. He, like Schweitzer, was born in Alsace. He had an air about him that was both formal and intense. And that evening, with words that rang out like hammers of light striking sheets of shadow, he teased out a brilliant thread woven through the history of Germany and the German language. Going back through the centuries, he traced the journey of a long struggle to resist the shadows being cast over the world—*Weltverfinsterung*. He gave new life and meaning to the engagement of German poets and intellectuals, citizens of the world who rose up against the imprisonment and obscurantist manipulations of thought and thus of language, against the gradual and arrogant perversion of the German language, whose path he mapped up until the dark era of Nazism.

As the winter night fell outside, in that small, virtually empty room, he read a poem out loud. One of Brecht's last poems, written shortly before his death in 1956:

SCHWIERIGE ZEITEN

Stehend an meinem Schreibpult
Sehe ich durchs Fenster im Garten den Holunderstrauch
Und erkenne darin etwas Rotes und Schwarzes
Und erinnere mich plötzlich des Holunders
Meiner Kindheit in Augsburg
Mehrere Minuten erwäge ich
Ganz ernsthaft, ob ich zum Tisch gehen soll
Meine Brille holen, um wieder
Die schwarzen Beeren an den roten Zweiglein zu sehen

Standing at my desk
Through the window I see the elder tree in
    the garden
And recognize something red in it, something black
And all at once recall the elder
Of my childhood in Augsburg.
For some minutes later I debate
Quite seriously whether to go to the table
And pick up my spectacles, in order to see
Those black berries again on their tiny
    red stalks.[1]

This was my first encounter with Brecht, and it saved my life. Because that is what poetry is: a human voice that can save you. And, in a way, it was also my first introductory lesson in German. The German that Brecht forged, as we would say of metal under the blacksmith's hammer, in order to wrench it out of the darkness. He did this, principally, through the *gestus*,[2] the linchpin of his entire approach as a man of the theater. A word that means both gesture and showing, demonstration, in the mathematical sense. The *gestus* of the man who, from stillness, begins to move in his body and in his mind, as though emerging from darkness into light, from the confused notions of the real to clear-eyed differentiation, expressing the slow gesture of his decision, the moment of freedom: to choose or not to choose. To bridge that abyss, step out of the darkness, resist, in and through language. To choose to resist—this was the message of that memorable evening. To work on Brecht's poetry was to work at the very root of thought, image, and music, at the root of what is perceptible and rational. It was also, and perhaps primarily, to work on the *gestus* of his writing which creates a fundamental distancing, a "disorientation, an effect of strangeness"—*Verfremdung*—that allows us to see the familiar in the foreign, the foreign in the familiar, and thus to create a sanctuary, where you are no longer foreign but someone who is learning. From that moment, I approached his poems as if entering a workshop, where I learned to adjust words with the utmost rigor to meet implacable lexical and syntactic standards.

Translation became a tool of that apprenticeship. Translation, like practicing scales, learning to listen, that never-ending fine-tuning of nuance. Translation became the clay from which I would fashion my own interior language.

LEARNING TO BE AN INTERPRETER

My educational journey took me to the door of the Berliner
Ensemble, in the East Berlin of the 1960s. The door was
locked, for this was Berlin at the time of the Wall. I went to
the box office, and the magic word that unlocked the door
for me was Brecht's *Antigone*, the subject of my disserta-
tion. The embodiment of resistance, and first and foremost
Brecht's resistance to the Nazification of the German language. He based his play on Hölderlin's translation, which
had been perverted and instrumentalized by the Nazis. It
was on the road of return from exile, in the little theater
in the town of Chur, in Switzerland, where he was waiting
and hoping—in vain—for permission to settle. He and his
wife Helene Weigel and the actors who made up their small
company were working on the diction of this text in order
to reappropriate their language after fourteen years' exile in
several different countries: France, Denmark, Finland, the
Soviet Union, and the United States. In order to give Germans the possibility of listening to their language again, a

de-Nazified German language in a production that was also de-Nazified.

That first morning, the woman from the box office showed me to the rehearsal room. Helene Weigel was expected any minute; she had gone to the ministry to complain about the shortage of toilet paper in nursery schools. She came in. She was dressed in black, upright, and somewhat aloof, but utterly present for each person. She showed me into her office. Or rather, she welcomed me, almost without words, but with a gesture of hospitality. Yes, that is definitely what it was, that is the word that sums up my encounter with Helene Weigel: hospitality. She immediately gave me permission to attend every rehearsal and to share the company's meals in the canteen. But since I had a grant for a university residence in the West, every night after the performance I had to cross over "to the other side," which meant traversing long dark corridors, endless verifications at the equally dark checkpoint, waiting on the deserted platform, the empty S-Bahn. So one day I plucked up the courage to ask Helene whether on performance nights I could sleep in a corner of the theater, in a chair, on a banquette—anything rather than that nightmare, the Wall, after dark. The Wall that infiltrated our nights, infiltrated our lives. The madness of men. She picked up the phone and found me a place to stay, right next door, with one of her old friends.

It was Helene Weigel who created the role of Antigone, in Chur, in 1948. She was supportive of my work and gave me access to the archives that were kept in Brecht's shabby old apartment. I was twenty. One evening I saw her play Mother Courage on the stage of the Berliner Ensemble, and when I heard her voice, with its diction that did not appropriate the text but set it at a remove, enabled it to be heard, to be "grasped" in that distance; when I saw the *gestus* of this woman, so delicate and strong, so intense and present, pain and dignity etched on her face, who raised herself up and gave us to see and understand that she had learned a different way of living and fighting from her son—this was the point at which I knew that I had not made that long journey in vain. And crossing the police checkpoints at the Wall in the grey dawn had not been in vain either.

Helene Weigel did not interpret, she was the interpreter. A magnificent lesson in the meaning of translation.

THE PRICE OF A LETTER

It was an evening during another winter, the one that followed the crushing of the Prague Spring, when I discovered a little book of poems, the unrefined color of brown parcel paper, that had been published in West Germany. The title on the cover was printed in dark green letters: *Sensible Wege*. It was a volume of poems by an East German poet, Reiner Kunze, who was banned in his own country, a friend and translator of the greatest Czech poets, who were at the time also banned, censored, and imprisoned: Milan Kundera, Jan Skácel, Vladimír Holan.

> *It is so easy to find the path that leads to our house.*
> —*Jan Skácel*

THE PATH TO YOUR HOUSE

It was so easy to find the path that leads to your house

. . . .

Pushing darkness
ahead of them
they strayed.
They camped
on the bridges
and instead of the axles
they heard men groaning in their sleep.

Now it is hard to find the path to your house.

In these times of solitude and solidarities, the price of a
letter that gets past the censors:

THE POSTMAN

Day after day
bringing
hope
with each step
creating an arch
between two shores with no bridge.

The postman
day after day
knocking on people's doors
but not allowed inside.

In these times . . .

In these times of solitude and solidarities: translation, a hand reaching from one shore to another where there is no bridge.

THE WEIGHT OF A WORD

Sensible Wege. The collection takes its title from one of the poems, a poem utterly limpid in its simplicity, written in everyday language, in the same rigorous German that bears Brecht's stamp. A precise and intricate language, leaving no chink for the slightest ambiguity either in its use or in its meaning. This was the language of Reiner Kunze, the East German poet, born in 1933 into a family of miners. But in a departure from this "realist" language was the word *sensible*—a word encompassing heart and spirit, "radar beneath the linden"[1]—a word in which collective history was refracted through the prism of an individual history. To translate this prism-word I needed much more than a dictionary; I had to take the risk of reaching out and questioning, of confronting the poet's very different reality. His reality, which was so foreign to me.

And so I set off for the town of Greiz, where Reiner Kunze lived, to meet him, to see his life, his street, his modest home in a drab apartment block under the constant surveillance of the Stasi. In the small living room lined with books where he had his desk, I listened to him explain, with words and silences, everything he had invested in the word *sensibel*:

SENSIBLE WEGE

Sensibel
ist die erde über den quellen: kein baum darf
gefällt, keine wurzel
gerodet werden

Die quellen könnten
versiegen

Wie viele bäume werden
gefällt, wie viele wurzeln
gerodet

in uns

FRAGILE PATHS

Fragile
is the earth above the springs: no tree should
be felled, no root
pulled up.

The springs might
dry up.

How many trees
are felled, how many roots
pulled up
within us?[2]

I listened to the poet read, alert to his intonations and
facial expressions. In the tiny blue kitchen, I was con-
scious of his precarious everyday life, the futile wait
each morning for letters that would never arrive, and the
unflagging, worried solidarity with his friends, the poets
of Prague and Moravia, reduced to silence or to exile—
all those lives now under threat after the crushing of the
Spring. Everything here spoke to me of that word *sensibel*, whose meaning I was slowly beginning to grasp, its
roots in the poet's language, both his languages: that of his
childhood and that of the Czech poets. His childhood language, drawn from the traditional songs his mother sang
as she worked, and the language drawn from the tradition
of the poets who had influenced him, from Walther von
der Vogelweide, Andreas Gryphius, Matthias Claudius,
Hölderlin, Heine, Rilke, and Peter Huchel, simultaneously
evoking that other and same line of poets annihilated by
the abstraction of German: Heinrich von Kleist, Jakob
Lenz, and Georg Büchner—*ausgegliedert*, all those who

had been "proscribed, rejected," and had died as a result. It was actually during that time of indoctrination, in 1950s East Germany, that the young poet first encountered the Czech language, which had been repressed and subjugated for two hundred years after the victory of Bavaria over Bohemia at the Battle of White Mountain in 1620. Intellectuals adopted the German language; it was thanks to ordinary people that Czech had survived over the centuries. It survived as the language of songs and poems, of myths and religious texts. The language of poetry, containing an infinite number of symbol-words, "songlike" names (*liedhaft*). Today it remains rooted in the everyday. It opened up in Reiner Kunze his own inner language, at the time repressed and almost forbidden. In a surprising dual movement, like the scoop that draws water from a field and pours it over neighboring furrows, he drew from the lines of the greatest poets of Prague and Moravia the rediscovered words of his interior language, with which he would later translate their poems in return.

Within the aura of this poetic language, the word *sensibel* resonated like an ultraprecise seismograph. I suggested translating it as *fragile*, I could hear that it sounded right.

Returning to the other side of the Wall after the Kafkaesque police formalities at the Friedrichstrasse checkpoint, I smuggled back the word I had come to seek.

IN THE URGENCY OF THE PRESENT

Thirty years later. The house beside the Danube, from which on a clear day you could see the treetops of the forest of Bohemia. The poet's window looked out onto the bends of the river. The opposite shore was already Austria. Wooded slopes where grey herons alight. It was at this confluence of three rivers, in this land of borders, that Reiner Kunze found refuge when he had no alternative but to leave East Germany.

On this borderland, he dug and planted one of the fragile sequoia saplings that his friend Alexander Graf von Faber Castell had brought back with him from Canada, dreaming they would grow into trees that would defy all temporal and spatial borders for a thousand years, acting both as witness to the enduring power of nature and as resistance to insane human threats. On this same borderland, the poet planted a young linden tree with broad leaves, the variety that soars like a canopy and for centuries has sheltered the memory of so many legends and songs and an entire part of the life of the ordinary people of his country.

On this August morning in 1998, the poet is describing the stony deserts of Namibia from where he has just returned. As I listen to him, I look through his photos of jagged crests and children's bare feet. Extending those stony deserts to the horizons of our society, the poet rails against the petrification that is gradually turning hearts and minds to stone, stoking insensitivity, the first step toward making barbarism possible. Through this word— *unsensibel* (insensitive)—the word *sensibel* suddenly takes on a whole new dimension, like a sinister echo, like an upside-down reflection in murky waters. The poet's words, spoken in the urgency of the present, carve out a space in the language of poetry, a space where the pulse of history beats. I suddenly recall those "fragile paths." And this morning, exactly thirty years to the day after the crushing of the Prague Spring, I have no option but to retranslate those words as "sensitive paths."

At that moment, I understood translation both as risk-taking and as continual re-examination, of even a single word—a delicate seismograph at the heart of time.

INTERIOR EXILE

During those autumn days when I was in Greiz interrogating the word *sensibel,* Reiner Kunze was invited to give a reading in a church in the town of Halle. The vast nave and the side aisles were packed. The Stasi were present, but this was one of the only places where the poet could not be banned. There was silence while Kunze read, interrupted by bursts of applause. This was more than listening, this was genuine understanding. As if the poet were giving people back their own words. For the duration of one evening, he was no longer excluded, banished, immensely alone.

Back in Greiz, Reiner Kunze picked up his telephone to call a good friend, a poet, also suffering. Solidarity between poets. The line crackled. On the other side, the plains swept by the first wintry north winds, the dark forests and the platforms of interminable waiting. The line crackled. On the other side, the no-man's-land of surveillance, suspicion, and informers. No-man's-land, a territory devoid of all humanity, where the poet's words are banned. Words, which come to life only when they ring forth, when they are shared like the bread of hospitality, now banned from being heard. The line crackled but Reiner Kunze's voice reached out, like a hand outstretched. Many years later, I found traces of that voice in the Stasi's files—tapped, stigmatized, blackened like sullied snow. A fragile connection.

The elderly poet Peter Huchel, who had been on the other end of the line that day, was waiting for me in the bleak solitude of his childhood home in Wilhelmshorst, near Potsdam. In the forests surrounding the lakes of the Spree. Home-root of his poetry, where every patch of light, every shadow, every window is a world in itself. And at the same time the home-crossroads where for decades he produced the magazine *Sinn und Form* (Sense and Form), which published so many poets, writers, and thinkers from every corner of the world, including Romain Rolland, Elio Vittorini, Charles-Ferdinand Ramuz, Federico García Lorca, Nazim Hikmet, Yannis Ritsos, Bertolt Brecht, Paul Celan, Ernst Bloch, Nelly Sachs, Jean-Paul Sartre, and Sean O'Casey. A meeting place for hearts and minds. Huchel had founded it amid the euphoria, openness, and optimism of 1948. He edited the magazine and kept it alive through thick and thin, unswervingly supported by his friend Brecht, until his dismissal when the Wall was built in 1961 and he found himself excluded from all intellectual and social life. Lands of memory and of banishment.

We walked in the mist shrouding the trees in his garden. Lands of imprisonment become lands of the universal through the power of poetry. The voice of the poet, deep and low, so restrained and wounded that it seemed to be speaking only to the deserted paths. In this internal exile, every morning was precarious. Poetry was his recourse and place of ultimate resistance, his inner country.

Is the frozen river
Still breathing faintly
Through the throat of the reed?[1]

As I worked closely alongside the poet to hone my translations, I listened to the silence of the empty house echoing through his words, the murmur of the tall maples "where the stigma(ta) of autumn burn(s)." I learned the accents of an interior language. A language of poetry experienced and shared at the source itself, the very place where it is under threat.

THIS UNIVERSAL LANGUAGE

It was the time when B-52s were dropping their bombs on the leper colonies and bridges of North Vietnam. Forests defoliated. Children's flesh burned by napalm, decimated by shrapnel and fragmentation bombs. In the context of the intense and urgent mobilization against this war, my dream of finding and giving voice to the poets of that country—so close and yet so far away—seemed ludicrous. I set off on a quest, with little idea where I was heading or how to go about it. I made my way up to the top floor of the Musée de l'Homme, where the library was housed, that unique, irreplaceable haunt which we knew was already under threat. Memory of the world, at that time still alive with the memory of resistance,[1] until it was dismantled when the Musée du Quai Branly was built. It housed a rich collection of Vietnamese literature, but the existing translations all dated from the French colonial period. I left with my notebook full of jottings in the margins, but all the pages blank.

In this maverick quest of mine, I received rare and genuine encouragement from one of the greatest mathematicians of his time, Laurent Schwartz. He was just back from North Vietnam, where he had been on a mission as vice president of the Russell Tribunal and as an academic, to bear witness to the resistance carried out during the American bombardment. He was a generous and empathetic person who paid close attention to the most fragile and endangered beauties of this world, and was also a highly expert and keen collector of butterflies from each of the continents he visited. He understood that poetry, like mathematics, lives and is part of the universal language of human intelligence and sensibility.

But where was I to find the voices of today's Vietnamese poets? In the shelters to which the children had been evacuated, in the trenches, the jungle, or the prisons?

LIKE A LETTER

It all began in a modest room in the Latin Quarter that
served as a meeting place for the fact-finding missions
of the Russell Tribunal. All? I mean my encounter with
Vietnamese poetry. The room was buzzing like a hive; a
delegation of Vietnamese had just arrived from the north
of the country and the jungles of the south to provide
eyewitness accounts. Over the course of these meetings,
trust and friendship developed between the Vietnamese
passing through and the Paris Conference delegates. We
began talking to one another about the important things
in life: children and their evacuation, separated families, illness, mourning, love . . . I discovered poems written in the
chinks within disasters. Poems which each person, even so
far from their country, carried with them as they trod the
paths of life and danger, never letting go of those little notebooks copied out by hand, sewn and cut to fit perfectly into
a jacket pocket. Like a letter never sent, forever received.

"I HAVE A DREAM"

In the heat of our discussions about poetry, my Vietnamese friends asked me if I would be prepared to leave France to be part of a project taking shape in Hanoi, whose purpose was to confront McNamara's declaration that the US would "bomb 'em back to the stone age" with the testimony of a culture that was several thousand years old. A crazy project in a country constantly under bombardment—to publish in French, for the first time since independence, a vast anthology of Vietnamese literature. To answer McNamara's threat with poetry.

TWO LINES FOR EACH LINE OF VERSE

The instigator of the project was Nguyen Khac Vien, a doctor whose many activities included organizing the evacuation of children during the bombings, running the foreign-language publishing house he had founded in Hanoi, and teaching his breathing method to patients suffering major trauma in the capital's hospital, as well as translation and numerous writing ventures in Vietnamese and French. After studying medicine in Hanoi and then Paris, where he defended his thesis in 1941, he was a patient in the Saint-Hilaire du Touvet sanatorium near Grenoble, initially for six months in 1942 and then again from 1943 to 1950. There he came into contact with the French Resistance. He went on to organize the resistance against the French colonial forces waging war in Indochina while helping and treating his fellow Vietnamese who had been commandeered and brought to France when the "phony war" broke out and then sent to detention camps for foreigners. Between 1940 and 1945, the three sanatoria of Saint-Hilaire became extraordinary hotbeds of debate and political engagement, taking in students with tuberculosis and at the same time offering sanctuary to young people dodging the Service du Travail Obligatoire,[1] as well as Resistance fighters in hiding. One can imagine the richness and intensity of the conversations and discussions between all those young sanatorium patients, among them Roland Barthes, Max-Pol Fouchet, Georges Canetti, and Emmanuel Mounier. Vien had a perfect knowledge of the French language and culture, and it was during those years in the sanatorium that he studied Western and Eastern philosophies and developed his own breathing technique based on yoga. It enabled him not only to survive with half a lung but also to continue his multiple pursuits once he returned home in 1963, after being expelled from France because of his political activities—which did not prevent him from winning the 1992 Prix de la Francophonie awarded by the Académie Française.

In 1971 he invited me to Vietnam to work with him on the planned anthology.

During the two years of preparation, I studied the language with the help of an entire team of Vietnamese, some of whom had been living in Paris for many years, others, young students exiled by the war. For the grammatical structure, a linguist who had just completed a research project under the supervision of Noam Chomsky; for the accents and diction of this tonal language, a musician and composer; to understand the music of verse and cantillation—that monotonous chant—my master, the musicologist Tran Van Khe; to teach me to read and speak, a recently arrived refugee woman student from Saigon. Once a week, I'd go to the studio of the sculptor Diem Phung Thi, who had invented what she called her "global poetry immersion method." She came from the Hue region. South Vietnam was her country, the inspiration and the stuff of her work. Everything she carved, drew, traced, cut out, all the materials she worked with—wood, clay, marble, bronze—everything was an expression of her country. So too were the clothes, the embroidered and woven items she wore, the aromas of the refined dishes she cooked with Diem, her husband. The first words she taught me were the Vietnamese for "native land": *dat nuoc*—land (and) water. Two words which opened up a whole different world. Is there any simpler, more concrete expression, any term more deeply rooted in human geography and which is rendered in French as *patrie*—fatherland? At the same time, she introduced me to poetry, my first poem in Vietnamese: "*Mien Nam*" ("The South") by the great poet To Huu. He was also born in Hue, where, at the age of nineteen, he was arrested and sent to a penal colony under the French. Diem Phung Thi opened a small volume of his poems, so little that it fitted into her hand, and she read and chanted in a low, slightly husky voice. Syllable-words whose modulation made the meaning resonate. I approached this first poem as if it were a letter addressed in turn to a friend, a loved one, a child. The first Vietnamese words of poetry I discovered were words of tenderness, of nostalgia, evoking—invoking—a country amputated, torn apart, a missing country, an absent country:

> *Nếu tâm sự cùng ta, bạn hỏi*
> *Tiếng nào trong muôn ngàn tiếng nói*
> *Như nỗi niềm nhức nhói tim gan?*
> *—Trong lòng ta hai tiếng: Miền Nam!*

> If, in hushed tones, you ask me, friend
> which single word out of a thousand
> opens up a wound inside me
> in my heart two words: The South![1]

This poem was written in December 1963, at the beginning of the American military escalation. I barely realized at the time the dimension not only of the war but also of the mobilization, as conveyed in those few, delicate words.

I arrived in Hanoi the day after the city had been under heavy bombardment by B-52s. Nguyen Khac Vien was waiting for me at the Gia Lam airport which had been partially destroyed. He had just finished the translation of *The Tale of Kieu*, the great epic poem by Nguyen Du. Right at the beginning, in his preface, he formulated the translation principle that was to inaugurate my apprenticeship in this utterly new context: "Staying faithful means first and foremost seeking to recreate the work's humanity, its universality." An approach that meant liberation from all forms of exoticism, appropriation, and the cultural and spiritual annexation characteristic of the translations produced under colonization.

The first day, mingling with Hanoi's early-morning crowds, I cycled past the Bach Mai hospital, which had been almost entirely destroyed in the bombing of December 22, 1972, that had killed twenty-eight members of the medical team. When I reached the publishing house, I found there was a shortage of paper but, toward evening, someone brought a bundle of beige-colored sheets that were rough, soft, and thick and which soaked up ink: work could begin.

I drew lines on each page, two lines for each line of verse: the top line for the first, elementary reading of the words, the bottom line for getting to the root of the source word by excavating the poems. I worked alongside the great poet Xuan Dieu, whom I had chosen as my comrade in poetry. He taught me to write on the bottom line the hidden layers of each word, the memory, the implicit allusions of an entire social imaginary, each time placed in the context of the life and history of a people. The bottom line was for the subterranean waters of poetry in the most everyday words, the top line for the customary meaning.

For example, for the word *duyen*:

Top line: *duyen*—attachment

Bottom line: love desired by the loved one
    love sworn for eternity
    bond of the soul that attaches one to the other
    nuptials—karma—fate

Top line—the usual dictionary definition: "attachment."
Underneath, Xuan Dieu opened up another lexicon, drawn
from *The Tale of Kieu,* the epic that was so popular that
women street vendors would put down their yokes at the
entrance to Hanoi's old theater and, barefoot, chewing
their betel, recite the lines under their breath from memory, along with the actors, following the silken skein of the
beautiful Kieu's life. The word *duyen* means, all at once,
"loved and desired by the loved one," "love sworn for eter-
nity," "bond of the soul that attaches one to the other," and
"nuptials—karma—fate." One word that contains an entire
world of resonances rooted in eighteenth-century feudal-
ism. And written on the bottom line, the words of the poet
Xuan Dieu, a slender brushstroke expressing karma, the
fate that seals the love known as *duyen.*

From that moment, translation came to mean learning to
listen to the silences between the lines, to the underground
springs of a people's hinterland.

FROM SHORE TO SHORE

December 1973, 17th parallel, the liberated zones of South Vietnam. A grey, humid light in a landscape of ruins, trees uprooted, shattered, a moonscape after the shelling by the B-52s. The road, an immense gaping hole in the misty rain of that winter dawn. A bridge, bombed so many times, mended and rebuilt so many times, on the opposite shore of this devastated place, a ghost village. Barefoot in the freezing mud the villagers have tied, braided, and knotted the wires collected along the McNamara Line, a gigantic electric fence erected to divide the country in two.

In the evening, I joined a vigil in the South, alongside men and women of the Resistance huddled around an oil lamp, shivering under layers of shirts and frayed cotton jackets. Someone had brought an old string instrument, made one night in a shelter from a gourd split open by the thunder of the giant bombers. Inside the makeshift shack, a voice rose up, another voice responded in an alternating song from the rice fields, the swaying of the buckets, echoes, and calls beyond the fields and the dykes—songs of life, love, and longing, popular chants mixed with cantillations of To Huu's lines:

Hỡi rừng sa mộc, khóm dừa xanh
Hỡi đồi cát trắng rung rinh nắng
Hỡi những vườn dưa đỏ ngọt lành![1]

Casuarina forests,
Groves of green coconuts,
The shimmering of the white dunes
where the sun trembles,
garden of watermelons with red honey!

I hear the song of the trees over this treeless land, the song of the trees in this time of napalmed villages, of defoliated forests.

That night, as we made our way down the narrow, potholed street in the dim starlight to fetch some water, a little intoxicated by the evening, I recited some lines by Brecht to the friend walking with me, a woman who had known prison as a resistant and had been separated from her children for years:

What kind of times are they, when
a talk about trees is almost a crime
because it implies silence about so many horrors?[2]

I tried to explain these lines, written by the poet during his years in exile, and what they say of his resistance to Nazism as a writer—but for her, for her people, the trees, the fragrance of the rice fields, of the flowers in the night, it was all part of the life forces, in no way different from commitment and resistance—quite the opposite.

If translation is building a bridge between two foreign shores, I realized that night how important it is for each one of the piles to be firmly anchored.

BYWAYS

September 1973, Tay Phuong Pagoda. Very slowly they climbed the two hundred or so steps up the Phat Tich hill, on top of which stood the pagoda. I have a clear image in my mind of the surrounding rice fields, and in the court-yard the little group of Vietnamese wearing dark green trousers and shirts. Against the wishes of my minders, we started a conversation. They came from a sanatorium in the Hanoi area and were on an excursion. Among them was a man with a gaunt face and the intense look of a person who has witnessed things that set him apart from others. His name was Cach, and he had recently been freed under the Paris Peace Accords after nineteen years in the prisons and penal colonies of South Vietnam, including the tiger cages of Pulo Condore. He had been arrested in 1954—just after the Geneva Conference, in his village south of the 17th par-allel where he was a farmer—because he campaigned for the country's reunification.

In the penal colonies and prison, he learned to read and write. With the help of Nguyen Khac Vien he was given permission to meet me at the publishing house. There he copied out for me from memory fragments of anonymous poems, individual voices that had become collective voices, which had circulated clandestinely at Pulo Condore:

IN THE TIGER CAGES OF PULO CONDORE (1958–1964)

. . . .
Generations and generations of men and blood and
     broken bones,
of flesh in shreds, of wounded feet.
Over the years, so many white tombstones
to make a road bordered with casuarina trees.[1]

Winter 1973. Thanks to Nguyen Khac Vien I was given permission to interview To Huu as part of the book project I had been dreaming of since I first read his poem "The South," in which he wrote about his journey as a revolutionary and a poet. We had three conversations, all in one of the Central Committee's vast meeting rooms. By that time he was no longer the barefoot young poet hidden by farmers and living and fighting among the most deprived and oppressed. He was a member of the politburo in charge of ideology and culture. I asked him how he reconciled writing poems that resonated with his people and driving around in a curtained limousine. He laughed and we set to work. I had only my notebook in which to write everything down, to ensure that nothing was lost.

After our first interview, I insisted on two conditions that would make it possible for me to complete the task of transcribing and translating. The first condition: that the poet Xuan Dieu work with me on this project and not an official in charge of poetry. And the second condition: that To Huu allow me, with his agreement each time of course, to select only poems that would still resonate in a hundred or a thousand years' time. In other words to reject those that were purely of the time and politically motivated, or rather those that were ideological and not true to his interior voice, his authentic, unassailable voice that touched a universal human chord. Prune the dead wood and only keep the living branches. The book was published in Paris. But we were never able to meet again in Hanoi.

To Huu was eighteen when he wrote the poem below dedicated to Nguyen Chi Dieu, who was then party secretary for the Central Region and had just returned from Pulo Condore, suffering from tuberculosis. To Huu visited him in the hospital, and from that day the noose began to tighten around the neck of the young poet, who was arrested soon after.

NHỮNG NGƯỜI KHÔNG CHẾT

Anh với tôi giữa bốn tường vôi lạnh
Lặng nhìn nhau, lựa phải nói năng chi!
Anh nghe thu rứt lá gọi đời đi
Tôi thấy cả một mùa xuân bước lại.
Anh là một thuỷ thủ già vững tay lái
. . . .
Chiều hôm nay, trên bãi đá chơ vơ
Tôi đứng ngó thuyền anh trơ xác chết
. . . .
Chết hay không, nhân loại, những linh hồn
Đã từng đau khổ lắm, đã tiêu non
Tất cả máu củn một thời trai trẻ
Để đem lại cho Người ngày mới mẻ?[2]

THOSE WHO DO NOT DIE

Between the four bare, cold walls
you and I look at one another in silence. There is no
    need for words.
You hear autumn shedding leaves, withdrawing the
    lifeblood
I watch an entire spring walking toward us
. . . .
Tonight—on the headland of solitary stones
I stand watching your boat laid bare, put to death—
. . . .

Do they die, oh you men of the earth! The souls
who have suffered so greatly, and given before it is
    time
all the blood of their youth
to bring you a new dawn?

"Yes! In prison, too, you find the time, there's nothing else
to do," To Huu told me. "To console yourself you write
poetry, in your head, in your mind, and then you learn it
by heart. . . . Sometimes I would write on the prison walls
with a pin, in tiny letters on the whitewash, but then they
painted all the walls and everything was erased. You could
say I lost a lot of poems in the prisons. When I was in the
cells I had no friends, no neighbors, no readers. So it really
was 'art for art's sake' [*laughs*]—purely individual, to forget
the days. . . . People slipped me green leaves, banana leaves,
and leaves from other species you find here, like the tropical
almond. Smooth, thick leaves, and then with pins, I wrote
on them. It was legible, very legible. No need for chemical
products—nice, thick, green leaves were all I needed. And
it came out a very pretty purple-black color. And the prisoners who worked outside gave the leaves to friends who
were waiting for them. Those were my first publications,
my first copies: branches, an entire branch, small, but with
lots of leaves. That way, it's public. A branch . . . A branch
with green leaves! It's innocent! Inoffensive! A branch that
is both poetry and politics."

Translation is also about taking the byways that lead to distant places. The ultimate refuge: poetry as the language of survival, of unassailable liberty.

SILENT SHELLS

For a soundboard, a small plank of *ngo dong* wood, the other two of *trac*; for a vibrator, a flexible tube made from a curved bamboo rod or from a slender horn; for a resonator, a small gourd or simply a coconut shell; to hold the single string, a wooden peg; and to release the harmonic sounds, the thin point of a bamboo stem, or the index fingernail of the right hand. This is the monochord, the instrument of the itinerant blind musicians. A poignant, haunting modulation of the syllable-words of this wordless voice, each one based on a six-tone scale. There is no term that can translate the breath-chant, the double silken thread of the cantillation it interweaves with the human voice. This is the soul of Vietnamese poetry. Nothing to do with the onomatopoeia or alliteration I had so proudly applied myself to producing in my early translations, believing, in my eagerness and ignorance, that I was rendering the music of a line by Tan Da—*La grue lentement prend son envol, puis à tire d'aile file au firmament* ("The crane slowly takes wing, then flies swiftly off into the firmament")—full of linguistic affectations which the monochord would later make me realize were mere empty shells, incapable of rendering the subtlety of a vast and entirely different kind of poetry.

At this extreme, translation can only retreat to the shore of absent words, then clutch at the shadow carried by the music inherent in those words. The poet To Huu and I came up with the idea of having the monochord accompany the speaking of the French text of one of his poems, the instrument's modulations expressing the harmonic sounds of the cantillation of the lines in its original language.

In order to experience the mystery of this poetry and its language as closely as possible, I wanted to learn to play the monochord. And so, with the help of Nguyen Khac Vien, a young musician from the conservatory came once a week to the little office of the publishing house to initiate me into its infinitely delicate and precise movements, as if into a secret. They had made me a monochord with what we had on hand, cobbling an old plug onto my small tape recorder to serve as a makeshift amplifier. I have kept the thin sliver of bamboo that my young female teacher cut for me, and still today, in each of the notes that it causes to resonate on that single cord, I listen intently to that wordless voice—a call that is both so distant and so close, so familiar and so foreign.

Is that not also a way to describe translation?

NEW VERSION OF AN ANCIENT TALE

That is the title of a poem written by Che Lan Vien in Hanoi during the B-52 bombardment of Christmas 1972. When I started working on the translation, the poet came to the publishing house and read it aloud to me. It is a long poem, as spellbinding as an ancient legend even though it was forged in the heat of the war.

Em ơi! Em có biết vì sao nhân loại thích truyện cho nhau
    từ đời này sang đời kia ngưng câu chuyện cổ?
Chỉ vì mỗi đội có thể thêm vào đấy những gì chưa có hôm
    qua.
. . . .
Phép lạ ngày xưa trong truyện có chị ở trong tay phù thủy,
Những phép lạ ngày nay là ở trong tay những người đi
    chain đất, trai tim tràn
Phép lạ là những người chết khát lại hóa thành ra suối.[1]

Little sister, do you know why humanity passes
 down
ancient tales, from hand to hand, from generation
 to generation?
It is so that each generation can add something that
 was not there yesterday.
 . . . .
The miracle of bygone days in the tales of long ago,
 used to be solely in the hands of sorceresses.
The miracle of today is in the hands of those who go
 unshod, their hearts bare.
The miracle is that those who are dying of thirst
 become springs.

That morning, listening to the poet's voice in our cramped
attic office, I understood that those words contained all the
hopes of a generation. His generation. Young people who
were twenty years old at the time of the August 1945 Rev-
olution and who gave their youth, their lives, for a dream
of independence and freedom. Thirty years of war. In his
slow, solemn voice, with its intonations of central Vietnam,
he evoked his journey of struggle and of poetry. He proudly
identified as a descendant of the Cham people and made a
point of recalling the destruction by the Vietnamese of the
Champa kingdom in the fifteenth century. Che Lan Vien
wrote and lived with the same steadfast voice, a rebellious,
generous voice that seized life and championed it against
all the odds:

Chúng hủy diệt. Và ta tồn tại.

They destroy
while we want to live[2]

He had sharp, watchful eyes, the gaze of a lookout, full of love for his fellow human beings. And a rebellious streak that kept him looking astonishingly young.

His mission was to preserve and transmit the cultural treasures of all peoples, all cultures—riches that transcend borders and are part of humanity's shared heritage. To preserve and transmit these treasure troves, built up with infinite patience, containing both the erudition and intimate knowledge of his people's wisdom and poetry, which he had collected in two school exercise books with faded purple covers held together with a couple of rusty staples. In the first exercise book, in his angular, slanting handwriting, he had copied out, in grey-blue ink, 365 *ca dao* (song-poems) in rhyming couplets, proverbs, and cantillated sayings, followed by a little personal anthology of the most beautiful anonymous folk songs. For each line, he had carefully underlined the rhythm and type of rhyme, every beat and threnody. In the second exercise book, he had made corresponding tables of all the types of rhymes and rhythms in Vietnamese poetry, creating a sort of mathematics of the ear. Thus he provided the keys to this musical system based on two types of words: *bang*—those without *ngang* accents, or with the *huyen* (grave) accent—and *trac* with four accents: *sac, nang, hoi, nga*. On the first page of the first notebook, he had written the following dedication: "It is through learning by heart that unconsciously—I repeat, unconsciously—you will understand the soul of the Vietnamese language, the structure, the rhythm, the grammar. Synthesis first, the elements afterward. This is my method, which I call the 'idiot method.'"

To preserve and transmit. Che Lan Vien was concerned for all minorities, but specifically Vietnamese minorities, for the survival of these mountain peoples and their cultures that were threatened with extinction. He was profoundly convinced that their legend-songs were part of the heritage of all humanity, and that by translating them into French we would help to preserve them. That was why he had come to the publishing house and asked me to help him carry out a project to translate three legend-songs from three different peoples of Vietnam: "The Great Crossing" of the Tay people, "The Song of the Daughter-in-Law" of the Hmong people, and "The Beautiful Om and the Young Bong Huong" of the Muong people. Nguyen Khac Vien gave me the go-ahead to work on this project at the same time as on the anthology, and he let us use a small office that opened onto the courtyard where we worked every evening on this intricate task. First of all, we needed to complete a word-for-word translation into Vietnamese, with the help of ethnologists from these three mountain peoples. Then, from that highly nuanced framework, as precise and detailed as possible, Che Lan Vien would help me construct one in French to which we would add suggestions and clarifications provided by our ethnologist friends. He brought to the task the whole of his culture and his in-depth knowledge not only of the French language but also of French poetry, which he had first come across and learned at French colonial school, poetry which had made such a profound impression on an entire generation, educating and, ironically, emancipating them. An entire generation of prerevolutionary youth. Then came the third stage: arranging all the notes, sounds, images, and narratives in such a way as to recreate the words, structures, and rhythms of an entire oral heritage. Those months and years of translation with Nguyen Khac Vien on the terrain of such a different culture, such a different reality, taught me to maintain a critical distance and a sense of discernment regarding the French tradition of translation that favored an exotic approach in which, as he put it, "weirdness and strangeness prevail over the human, where phoenixes and dragons hide men. . . . Exoticism arouses simply a sense of foreignness, without being able to communicate the emotions, the deeper feelings that inspire a work."

Nguyen Khac Vien had not only helped me to gather words and images which I could quite simply have transposed and enclosed within the static clichés of folklorists.

He showed me a different approach, a different way of being open to the world. He showed me that translating Vietnamese poetry had different requirements, that it was necessary, within the infinitesimal and the specific at the core of these words and images, to seek out—as close to the ground and to today's reality as possible—those elements that are universal, alive, still shifting. To do this, and with the modest (scant) resources available during the tough years between the never-ending peace negotiations in Paris and the last years of a drawn-out war, with its terrifying modern means of wreaking devastation, he found a way for me to spend time among the mountain peoples, sharing their day-to-day lives. I slept in their bamboo houses raised on stilts; I sat around the fire and shared the rice that had been pounded and cooked by the entire community, who gathered afterward to cantillate and, in the depths of night, give voice to these enduring, indestructible, and yet terribly delicate fragments of humanity's treasures.

Back in Paris, I was convinced that theoretical works would not provide the answers to my questions about forms of orality. As I dug deeper, investigating everything that was being done in these areas of research and study, I came across the work of a field ethnologist, Charles Joisten, whose entire focus was on the spoken word, the need to preserve the words of ordinary people, which at that time were not being recorded and so seemed destined to vanish from collective and individual memories. He had been living in the Alps for many years, carrying out his patient, meticulous, methodical work of gathering stories, legends, proverbs, adages, sayings, and the transmission of artisanal skills. I have warm memories of the generous welcome he gave me in his office at the Musée dauphinois in Grenoble, where he was a curator, where Jean-Pierre Laurent was putting together an exhibition about mountain peoples called *Gens de là-haut*. This was a pioneering exhibition based on a museographical approach that sited all the collected words within their social, economic, cultural, emotional, and environmental contexts. I spent many hours listening to his recordings, absorbing the rhythms and cadences of those words and voices, discovering an entire register of expressions, accents, and constructions.

It was like drawing a breath, the breath of an utterance that was both specific and universal.

> Little brother, wait no more.
> Speak out, let your voice sound.
> . . . .
> In ten generations,
> my story will be sung by the blind,
> so that hamlets and villages will hear,
> so that posterity will know.[3]

BRIEF POSTSCRIPTUM

At the bottom of a page, in the corner, right at the edge, Che Lan Vien had made a note in tiny handwriting, with a red ballpoint pen, as though it were a rough draft. He had jotted down four words whose significance he explained to me while we were talking about the etymology and roots of words:

thu: letter
tho: poetry

I found that pleasing—as if translating a poem, for me, was always a little like translating a letter, both exceedingly distant and infinitely close.

A SECOND GLASS OF LIGHT

It was a beautiful July day in the summer of 1974. The Provençal light, the rural road to the Isle-sur-la-Sorgue winding through the vineyards and lavender fields, and on the horizon, the blue crests of the Lubéron. The road, a bridge between the banks of the Sorgue, and a poet from Hanoi, Te Hanh. A poet from a country that had been at war for so many decades, who was excited by the great journey that translation represented for him. The day before I left Hanoi for a short holiday in France, he confided in me his dream that one day he might discover and translate some French poetry other than the official Hanoi canon—the poetry of Louis Aragon, Paul Éluard, Pierre Gamarra. I spoke to him of René Char:

Hurry
Hurry to transmit
Your share of marvel rebellion beneficence.[1]

It is snowing on the maquis, and hunting us down is
perpetually in season.[2]

And that was how I came to be driving down this road of
light on that July day. Past the Isle-sur-la-Sorgue, a little far-
ther on the left, his house, "Les Busclats," which I had been
looking forward to seeing for so long, suddenly came into
view. I pushed open the old gate. René Char, the embodiment of intelligence and humanity, came out to meet me.
I had not called to say I was coming—who, how would
I have introduced myself? There were no steps up to the
house. He showed me into the cool, dim, low-ceilinged living room and poured me a glass of Muscat de Beaumes de
Venise, whose golden glow was warm as the sun, even as it
exuded the exquisite coolness of mysterious subterranean
cellars. I had barely finished talking about the Vietnamese
poet, inseparable from his little bag full of books and his
mad dream to translate him, when René Char poured me a
second glass of light, left the room, and came back with his
hands full of poems. In delicate, elongated handwriting like
black cypresses straining in the mistral, he wrote words on
the flyleaves as if extending his hand in friendship and told
me to embrace his brother in poetry on his behalf.

I left with those treasures in my bag—or rather my
shepherd's satchel, because that little Provençal road
made me think of transhumance: the long, slow movement of the flocks to distant places, in search of the

greenest pastures, the low plains in winter and the high valleys in summer. All the ancient routes that have witnessed encounters and exchanges in all the dialects of the "umbrella language" of Provençal. So it is with the transhumance routes of translation, the slow and patient crossing of countries, all borders eradicated, the movement of huge flocks of words through all the vernaculars of the umbrella language of poetry.

Te Hanh, transported by writing that was both so foreign and yet so infinitely familiar, read with wonderment Char's dedications to him, steeped in the scents of Les Busclats. Char's poem emerged from this great journey into Vietnamese, as if it had been hewn from the earth of the rice fields:

LA LIBERTÉ

Elle est venue par cette ligne blanche pouvant tout
aussi bien signifier l'issue de l'aube que le
bougeoir du crépuscule

TỰ DO

Chi dên con duong trang kia
Có thê là dâu hiêu cua binh minh
Mà cung co thê là ngon dên cua hoang hôn[3]

LIBERTY

It came along this white line signaling either
the dawning day or the glow of dusk

Translation and poetry, a far-off encounter at the confines
of language, on the watershed. The essence of hospitality.

IN THE CRYSTAL-BLUE DUSK

Nelly Sachs: Jewish German-language poet—not the German of Mitteleuropa, but that of Berlin. Yet when I read her poems a voice spoke to me from elsewhere, a voice that was deeply familiar . . . It was years before I was able to access her deeply painful poetry, to edge close enough to imagine being able to translate it. This was in the 1990s; Nelly Sachs had died in exile twenty years earlier in Sweden. This was the first time I would be translating a body of work without being able to meet the poet—although I felt she spoke to me in a familiar language. I went to Stockholm, in search of personal memories of her from her fellow exiles, but I had no idea where to look for inspiration, nor where to settle down to undertake this long-term project.

A residency at the Collège International des Traducteurs Littéraires in Arles offered me a haven in the converted former sixteenth- and seventeenth-century hospital, the Hôtel-Dieu Saint-Esprit. The library is housed beneath the ceiling of what was once the main ward, with its massive beams. Its high windows look out over the small cloistered garden that has been restored to its original design, with its ancient trees and flower beds, a riot of Mediterranean colors and fragrances. It was in that former ward, at my desk, looking out onto the garden, that I began to feel that this truly was a place where it would be possible to capture the bursts of light and music of Sachs's poetry of disaster in the urgency of its time. I remember that late summer afternoon, as dusk was about to fall and the mistral had given the sky an extraordinary radiance. I was on my way back from a meeting at the offices of the publisher Philippe Picquier at Mas de Vert to discuss the content of the anthology of Vietnamese literature he was planning to publish that autumn. It included a selection of the poems I had translated in Hanoi with To Huu, Che Lan Vien, Te Hanh, and Xuan Dieu. Was it the voice of all those poet friends with whom I had journeyed across so many human landscapes and shared so many tears and joys? Was it the life force I had drawn from living among those people, in the intimacy of their everyday lives, sharing with them their poems and legend-songs, their sanctuaries? Whatever it was, in the clear blue of the intense dusk, I suddenly heard the secret murmur of Sachs's poetry infused with Hebrew calling to me. I suddenly felt, despite everything, a surge of faith in the indestructible light lodged within the human heart. I was ready to begin.

A SLIVER OF PLANE TREE BARK

"I am sending you something to help assuage the niggling doubts that sometimes assail us. It is a sliver of plane tree bark. Hold it firmly between your thumb and index finger and think of something good. But—I can't keep this from you—poems, and yours especially, are even better than slivers of bark." For me, that little sliver of Parisian bark, which Paul Celan slipped into an envelope addressed to Nelly Sachs, in a way reflects the writing in their letters. Concise, compact, dense. Breathless words, urgent and intense:

> Let us who are already free be the freest of all, the ones
> standing-with-you-in-the-light![1]

From now on translation would mean taking syntactical and semantic risks to convey the urgency and intensity of those languages of the extreme between two beings.

THE FOUR NOTEBOOKS

It was during the time of darkness, the grim years of the rise of Nazism in Berlin, the years that preceded Nelly Sachs's exile to Sweden, arranged thanks to some "righteous Germans," as she called them. She wrote to Ben-Gurion during the Eichmann trial, asking, "in the name of the righteous Germans," that Eichmann not be executed. She cited Abraham's prayer for Sodom: "Will you sweep away the righteous with the wicked? . . . What if there are fifty righteous people in the city? What if only twenty? What if only ten?"

It was during those years of persecution that Nelly Sachs discovered (or rediscovered?) her Judaism. Like a return—in Hebrew, *teshuvah*—to the roots of her inner self. "Like a return to her heart."[1] A return she made later on as a poet, using the language of the translation of the Hebrew Bible that Martin Buber and Franz Rosenzweig embarked on after the First World War. Sachs discovered their work at the beginning of the 1930s when she came across a copy of the Book of Isaiah that was circulating among her friends. Buber wrote in the preface to the 1954 edition: "Franz Rosenzweig (already silenced by illness) died on 10 December 1929. The last words he said to me just before he died were from the passage of Isaiah 53 about God's suffering servant." Nelly Sachs was deeply moved by this translation. Just at the time when the extermination of the Jewish people was taking hold in people's minds, and concretely in the camps, with a prescience that is perhaps unique to the poet, she started to inject into her own German language a whole new dimension, a new Scripture, infusing it with Hebrew and forging the language of her future poetry. This became the matrix for the entire opus that she was to produce during her exile in Stockholm, right up until her death. In the 1950s Hans Magnus Enzensberger wrote that "there is a life-saving quality about her language. When speaking, she returns to us, sentence by sentence, what we were threatened with losing: language. Her entire oeuvre does not contain a single word of hatred. To the persecutor and to everything that makes us accomplices or acolytes, she addresses neither forgiveness nor threats, neither curses nor revenge. There is no language for them. The poems speak only of what has a human face: the victims. That is what gives them their enigmatic purity. It is what makes them unassailable."

My translation of Nelly Sachs was a long-term project, for I had decided to translate her entire body of work. No doubt this sweeping perspective, the fact of contextualizing every single line, poem, and collection, is what led me to develop a method that was similarly long-term, a method suited to the specificity of Nelly Sachs's work and which I did not envisage applying to any other poet. It comprised a sequence of readings and different approaches that complemented each other and slowly wove the texture of the translation. Four notebooks gradually emerged corresponding to four writings—four re-writings. Four horizons. "Like four keys to this work," in Esther Starobinski-Safran's words. Without my realizing, Nelly Sachs led me every step of the way along a preexisting path that was the path of her inner identity, the language of her soul. And like an echo, this made the fundamental elements of the Bible's four levels of meaning resonate according to the Jewish tradition of exegesis—*Peshat*, literal meaning; *Remez*, allusive meaning; *Drush*, deeper meaning; *Sod*, secret, esoteric meaning—but modulated and developed in her work with differences and a freedom that derived from the precise nature of her poetry.

The first notebook. The first level of writing, which revealed the immediacy of this poetry inhabiting human time. I remember the first lines of the first poem of the first volume:

O the chimneys
On the ingeniously devised habitations of death[2]

I had not read beyond those very first words and already I felt a kind of vertigo: suddenly, in contrast to words that were immediately understandable, I stumbled over the word *sinnreich* (ingenious), freighted with all the perverse displays of which human intelligence is capable. I sensed that translating this word was going to require me to probe the darkest human depths, to embark on this "belief in transcendence through suffusion with pain, in the inspiritment of dust, as a vocation to which we are called."[3]

In the first notebook, in the initial unfolding of her poetry, I found kernels of images, allusions, and underlying meanings. Stripping away the bark and shining a light on them as if from within was going to be a long process, a journey through Sachs's entire body of work and many other layers of writing. I did not know yet that the fourth notebook was the one that would yield a key, reveal a coherence and an inner meaning, hidden beneath the seemingly obvious:

> O the night of the weeping children!
> O the night of the children branded for death!
> Sleep may not enter here.
> Terrible nursemaids
> Have usurped the place of mothers[4]

A stranger always has
his homeland in his arms[5]

🖎

MY DEAD LOVES

Your dreams now orphans
Darkness has shrouded the images
Dispersed in ciphers
Your language sings
. . . .

Your wandering legacy
begs along my shores

Unquiet
So very afraid
to grasp this treasure
with my humble life
        Myself custodian of fleeting moments
Heartbeats, adieux, death wounds[6]

The second notebook. The second level of reading, in which
an entire dimension of meaning was revealed through the
structures, the building blocks of Nelly Sachs's poetic language, marked and subtly enriched by her long acquain-

tance with Buber's writings in the German of the Galician Jews, and, above all, profoundly inspired by the Hebraic, Biblical German of Buber and Rosenzweig's translation of the Bible, which Esther Starobinski-Safran analyzes as follows:

The important thing, says Buber, is not the meter, but the articulation of the units, which are both breath-units and meaning-units. The important thing is to recreate the tension characteristic of the architecture of the ancient Hebrew syntax, the specific way Hebrew plays on words stemming from the same root, or which have a similar sound, whether they are in close proximity or far apart in the text. In the same way it is essential to reproduce the powerful rhythm of ancient Hebrew, which overrides any meter. Fundamentally, the message conveyed by the inevitable merging of sound and sense cannot be transmitted. Buber is anxious to reveal the "corporeality of the Biblical spirit" (*die Leiblichkeit des biblischen Geistes*), to rediscover the original sensuality beneath the shell of common abstractions, to free the translation from the common usage of words in everyday conversation or in the dictionary, which only gives a superficial meaning. The immediate signification is matched by a hidden meaning.[7]

How was I to render in French this foreignness, this shift inherent in Nelly Sachs's language, if not through a *dis*-location? Similarly with the rhythm of the words themselves—movements and nuances of separable and inseparable particles, including the countless uses of *ver* in infinite guises:

das Gebet zu finden
das die verstümmelten Silben zusammenfügt

  to find the prayer,
  which joins the mutilated syllables

Zeit der Verpuppung
Zeit der Vergebung
Verfallene mit dem Gesicht im Staub
verspüren schon den Schulternschmerz der Flügel
Wettlauf der Meridiane auf der Sternenhaut
Aderlass der Sehnsucht ins Meer der Verklärung

  Time of pupation
  time of remission
  ruined ones with their face in the dust
  already sense the shoulder ache of wings
  meridians race on their stars' integument

bloodletting of longing into the ocean of
transfiguration[8]

🖎

IN DER FLUCHT

An Stelle von Heimat
halte ich die Verwandlungen der Welt—

FLEEING

I hold instead of a homeland
the metamorphoses of the world—[9]

So it was too with compositions of names and participles:

soviel Samenkörner lichtbewurzelt

So many seeds of light

Nachtbehandschuht: gloved night
Mutterwasser: maternal water

And with the versification rhythm, a ballet of caesurae, and
"suitable pauses":

einatmend des Todes
dunkles Gewürz

inhale the musk of death

The unifying thread and hidden pulse of Sachs's poetics is the breath-meaning, breath-breathing, the breath that makes and gives sense. This is what the Swiss oboist Heinz Holliger was emulating in his breathless composition *Glowing Enigmas*, which he came to Stockholm to work on with Nelly Sachs in 1964.

NUR IM SCHLAF HABEN STERNE HERZEN

Ebbe- und Flut-Atem
üben mit den Seelen
die letzte Vorbereitung

STARS HAVE HEARTS AND MOUTHS

Ebb and flow of breathing
rehearses with souls
the last preparation.[10]

Ruach (breath) and *mayim* (water) are the elements running right through Nelly Sachs's poetry: air, wind, last breaths and the breath of life, sighs, spring, water, seas and oceans, rivers and eternal fountains, echoing the opening verses of Genesis:

Darkness was on the face of the deep
And the Spirit of God—*Ruach Elohîm*—moved upon
the face of the waters.

And characteristic of this Biblical dimension, her endless seeking:

If only I knew what the elements mean;
they strive to understand you, for everything points
always
to you; I can do nothing but cry[11]

This breath-*ruach* transforms the rhythm of her poetry, creating one long, sweeping psalm. A psalmodic breath, the essential difference between the cadences of Buber and Rosenzweig's Bible translation and Luther's prose translation.

It is in this extreme care to highlight every synonym, every word grasped and articulated not simply through repetition but in the expression of all its nuances and in the "understanding of etymologies," that Buber and Rosenzweig developed their Hebraic German, creating a new space for responsibility instead of being crushed under the weight of original sin.

So, for example, Luther translates the lines in Isaiah 1:4 as: *Weh dem sündigen Volk, dem Volk mit Schuld beladen* (Woe to the sinful people, to the people laden with guilt), while Buber and Rosenzweig remain close to the Hebrew roots and to the original syntactical articulation, opting for:

> *Weh*—term of lamentation, apostrophe, or address; "O"
> *wegfehlender Stamm*—lineage that loses-its-way
> *schuldbeschwertes Volk*—blame-laden people

Nelly Sachs's voice is articulated around the same appeal to the other, the same call for dialogue, for consciousness, for responsibility:

> Two hands, born to give,
> Tore off your shoes
> My beloved,
> Before they killed you.[12]

🖋

HANDS

The gardeners of death
. . . .
what did you do,

when you were tiny children's hands?
· · · · · · · · · · · · · · · · ·
You strangling hands,
was your mother dead,
your wife, your child?
So that all you held in your hands was death.[13]

The third notebook. This contains the intersecting links that Nelly Sachs weaves together with the great Jewish texts, using the language (and images, evocations, and echoes) of Buber and Rosenzweig's translation. In human words, in language that resonates with suffering and heartbreak, yet also with moments of light in the midst of times of disaster:

> If the voice of the prophets
> should pipe
> on the flute bones of the murdered children[14]

All the holy places and the great prophetic figures are invoked, voices called upon for help in those dark times:

DAVID

> built inns of night from the psalms
> for those left by the way

DANIEL

> Where are you terrible dreamlight?
> The uninterpreted signs have become too many—

SINAI

> Is there still an heir
> to the succession of them that trembled?
> Oh, may he glow
> in the crowd of them that do not remember,
> of the petrified![15]

And echoing this quest, rewritten in the depths of the abyss, a Song of Songs for a time of anguish:

> Constellation of the beloved
> extinguished by the hangman
> . . . .
> She searches she searches
> ignites the air with pain[16]

The fourth notebook. The final level of reading that loops back to the first level, the words now illuminated as if from within: "That is when the desire to discover the 'kernel' of the text is awakened, the desire to enter the text to extract its secret, the *sod*."[17]

In this notebook, the lines are imbued with a mystical aura, from the *Zohar* cycle:[18]

> The alphabet's corpse rose from the grave,
> alphabet angel, ancient crystal,
> immured by creation in drops of water
> that sang—and through them you saw

glinting lapis, ruby, and jacinth,
when stone was still soft
and sown like flowers.[19]

How was I to translate this untranslatable mystical radiance, to adhere as closely as possible to the poet's language? How was I to find the right words that would not betray those limpid images and tones, inspired by the words of the *Zohar*, which Nelly Sachs studied in Gershom Scholem's translation?

The light was a mouth that did not speak[20]

I found the inspiration for these words in Charles Mopsik's translation of the *Zohar*, in the astonishing quality he injected into the French language, the denotations/connotations "that brought out particular relations and unexpected connections." This is language that "goes beyond meaning, to signification," as he writes in his preface.

Translating, here, was about opening up a mysterious dictionary from which to extract something bold, it was about reaching the limits of understanding, risking going beyond the literal meanings of the words, in order to access their deep meanings.

Beyond the choices of syntactical construction—beyond the choices of verbs, adjectives, nouns, the particles' infinite nuances, and the risk of compound words—at the heart of this poem there remained, and remains, an aura of mystery.

For the first time in my work as a translator, I understood that "to translate," in a strange and unique way, could also mean "to interpret," in the sense of the verb *deuten*, which is how Buber and Rosenzweig translate the order that Pharaoh gave Joseph to interpret (*liftor*) his dream (Genesis 41:15). It is a task demanding both extreme rigor and distance, to enable each person to hear what is "beyond" the poem, what is written in the poem itself, that splinter of stellar light that Nelly Sachs wrenched from the darkness and infused into the devastated German language.

> In the snow
> the woman's halting gait
> betrays
> her secret
> servitude
> a budding and yet broken branch
> surrendered to the powers of Night.[21]

THIS LANGUAGE OF HOSPITALITY

We had just turned off one of those ancient mountain tracks winding from the nearby sheepfolds of La Crau to the distant pastures of the southern Alps and Piedmont. Our path ascended Mont Paon. As he made his way through juniper, rockrose, rosemary, shrub oak, and Aleppo pines, the friend who was my guide told me about a young Jewish ethnologist who was born in Odessa in 1884 into a family that came originally from Galicia, on the border of the Tsarist empire. One freezing-cold day when the first snows were falling, she arrived in Bessans, a village deep in Savoie, to live alongside the mountain dwellers and study their way of life. As we walked and I listened, I sensed that there was something more than just the appeal of glaciers and the beauty of the imposing peaks in this young woman's quest. The mountain path we were climbing was very steep. On reaching the summit, we suddenly saw, in the still night-blue distance, a magnificent rainbow stretching from the Alps to the sea, as the first rays of sunlight picked out one by one the stones of the ancient ruins around us. A constellation in which light triumphed over darkness. Those vast open horizons on that early morning hike were symbolic of my first encounter with Eugenie Goldstern, who had been driven out of Odessa by the pogroms of 1905, became a refugee in Vienna, and was murdered at Sobibór in 1942. She wandered that sweeping alpine arc, defying all borders, sharing, discovering, understanding, and describing the lives of people who lived in the most remote valleys, undeterred by frontiers from which she was pushed back more than once. Her writings, like glowing stones, also seemed somehow symbolic, revealing a capacity for wonderment before the simplest things, the empathy and respect she had for the humblest lives, the offerings from the person who arrives as a stranger. Those glowing stones that the Nazis sought to wipe out in the darkness of oblivion and ignorance.

A translation whose origins were at the meeting point of those paths of light, among the rockrose and the rosemary. It was like a slow victory over darkness as I restored a voice to the writings we had unearthed in libraries in London, Vienna, and Geneva, pulling them out intact from the ashes of catastrophe. To date these writings have not been republished in Austria.

A long journey through Eugenie Goldstern's writings, which recorded the minutiae of day-to-day lives in the villages, hamlets, and alpine pastures on the fringes and the shattered borders of Europe in the first quarter of the twentieth century. From the Balkans to Savoie, including the village of Bessans, burned down by German troops in the summer of 1944 and whose memory she had preserved in the research she undertook in the months leading up to the First World War.

It was a journey that covered a great distance but which lasted barely ten years in time, and was brutally curtailed in 1924 when Nazi ideologues took over the academic study of ethnology in Austria.

Eugenie Goldstern's geography is one of both exile and belonging, wherever humans are to be found. A geography rooted in the notion of complementarity, which I learned about over time under her mentorship. It was a profound lesson in humanism and in her pioneering approach to ethnography.

This complementarity came out of the comparisons she explored in time and place, through different approaches, as she sought to uncover meaning and investigate the enduring aspects of those vanishing worlds that continue to fascinate us so deeply today. It was evident in her comparative work on so-called "primitive toys" which she studied and collected in remote Swiss valleys in 1919 and 1920. She was looking into their links with religious objects, leaving it to future generations to pursue a line of thinking that went beyond the resources available to her at the time. There was the study based on the conversations she had on farms and in pastures, with children whose simple, everyday words she collected and scrupulously transcribed, words that bubbled up from their imaginations to name and describe their precious toy-objects and explain their use.

This notion of complementarity was integral to her language, which was both supranational—as Imre Kertész called that German without a territory: the German of Kafka writing in Prague, Paul Celan or Joseph Roth in Paris, Elias Canetti in London, and Stefan Zweig in Brazil—and at the same time the sanctuary of each dialect of the places she visited. She embraced and gathered with tireless rigor and precision the words and expressions of a particular valley, hamlet, or locality, and their variants on the other side of the mountain or the frontiers suddenly erected after the First World War.

How was I to translate this idea of complementarity, the comparatism of a language that weaves between the remotest places and is composed of all the nuances and preciseness of their idioms, sayings, and names across the Alps, from Slovenia to Savoie, from Piedmont to Tyrol, via the canton of Valais and Les Grisons? My research into the terms and my efforts to find appropriate translations took me first to the Ethnography Museum of Geneva, where Erica Deuber Ziegler and her team welcomed me and gave me access to the Georges Amoudruz collection of everyday objects of the Savoie mountain people, as observed by Eugenie Goldstern. But it was a monolingual approach. How was I to build a sort of topographical lexicon, with all the variants that depended on the locality and customs of each term placed in context?

The next phase of my search took me to Fribourg to visit Jean-Pierre Anderegg, an eminent ethnologist and expert on alpine habitats and their architecture. He undertakes most of his research in this bilingual canton, his adoptive home. A native German speaker, he writes and conducts his research in French and German and has a perfect knowledge of the terminology not only in both these languages but also in the plurilingual tradition of Switzerland; he knows the variants in Italian and Romansh. In accordance with the Swiss tradition of ethnography, he works in the field, studying habitats and ways of life, collecting terms and their variants in the dialects or patois of the four national Swiss languages. He adopts the *Wörter und Sachen* (Words and Things) process passed on to him by his master, Richard Weiss, incorporating it into a contemporary, cross-border anthropological approach.

There is a profound kinship in his methods with those of Eugenie Goldstern. I brought him a set of first editions of her collected works, which contain all the words she had gathered and conscientiously annotated and included. For example, her study of the houses of Val Müstair listed the local Rhaeto-Romance or Rhaetian vernacular terms she had identified. Jean-Pierre Anderegg knows not only how these are related to the terms of the dialects of South Tyrol and Friuli in northeast Italy but also both their German and French transcriptions and equivalent terms: French words whose topography he taught me to trace, taking into account variations in their usage according to geographical contexts and local customs. So, for instance, the word *maison* in Low-Valais means "kitchen," while the word *chalet* in French-speaking Switzerland reflects an entirely different social and cultural reality from the same word used in Savoie.

We set to work, and thanks to his multilingual skills and his knowledge of the areas involved, an entire vocabulary developed, creating a pathway into a French whose precise use I was able to pin down with the help of a small team of anthropologists, architects, veterinary surgeons, art historians, and botanists, and which I gradually realized would be "cross-pollinated" to reflect the language of Eugenie Goldstern, the way it was open to all the cultures she passed through and respectful of all the various differences and complementary knowledge. That German language, the crucible language of Mitteleuropa, which she made the language of her writing. That language on which the Nazi ideology had no grip, because it is a language of the mind, without a territory and without borders and with multiple affiliations. That language which she adopted, but from which she was exiled as early as 1924 when she found herself excluded from all fields of research, intellectual life, publishing, and science, once Arthur Haberlandt, ethnologist and Nazi, was made director of the Vienna Volkskundemuseum.

Translating that irreducible, unassailable German required a lengthy and meticulous process of engaging in a humanist approach employing the humblest particular to investigate universal human explorations in time and space. A long apprenticeship learning to listen to that language, so enriched by the vernacular of all the countries it traveled through, going with her, step by step, across all those territories. That was why, as I was finalizing my translation, I decided to set off for one of those very remote, high Swiss valleys where Eugenie Goldstern had roamed. I was a guest at the modest house, also a foundation, belonging to Professor Niederer, who was one of the very first ethnologists to visit Bessans and discover her work. It was only while I was finishing this translation, while I was staying in that little valley enclosed by a glacier, that I was able to understand the extent to which this language and this body of work had escaped, transgressing all the boundaries being put in place in interwar Europe.

I remember clearly how, one morning as the snows were melting, as I sat at the ancient table beneath the blackened beams, it suddenly dawned on me that the stranger was not the other, it was me. I was the one who had everything to learn, everything to understand, from the other. That was probably my most essential lesson in translation.

LANGUAGE OF CHILDHOOD

How poignant the early morning silence is over the village of Izieu, on the border of the Ain and the Isère regions. On the afternoon of April 6, 1944, two tarpaulin-covered trucks drove up the winding road to the orphanage where forty-four Jewish children were hiding. Under orders from Klaus Barbie, head of the Lyon Gestapo, they were on their way to arrest them—arrest these children's lives, their clamor. How poignant is this silence-emptiness, this silence-absence, as the morning mist lifts over the still sleeping village.

The child, at the heart of Nelly Sachs's work, the background key to her poetry, the common thread running through all her books.

We had organized a reading inside the old stone walls that had once sheltered the children, by the fountain where they used to play, now dry. And on hearing her poems echo among the exercise books still open at the page where time had stopped, among the letters and drawings torn from the tree of life, I realized that the language of her poetry is the language of childhood: strangled with pain and outrage and questions forever unanswered, she goes back in time and draws on the images, words, wonderment, and expectations of absolute trust:

> O the night of the weeping children!
> O the night of the children branded for death!
> . . . .
> Yesterday Mother still drew
> Sleep toward them like a white moon[1]

𝒦

> Always
> where children die
> stone and star
> and so many dreams become homeless.[2]

Language of childhood:
This is the language whose words Imre Kertész discovered intact in Auschwitz, impregnable word-acts, expressing a gesture of tremendous humanity, the actions of "a man, or rather a skeleton, who, I have no idea why, was only ever referred to as 'Teacher,'" who staggered toward the child "lying on the wooden contraption that passed for my stretcher" and risked his life to give him "a single issue of

cold rations" with words salvaged from the disaster: "You didn't imagine for one moment . . . ?"[3] Words of salvation for the child who no longer believed.

Language of childhood:
Words which Aharon Appelfeld, typographer of interior language, found in the depths of darkness, recasting and recomposing every single letter which he then placed inside the mold of his "new language." Words which "took root" in him and became his writing language.

The language-land of the soul.

NOTES

Unless otherwise noted, all translations are by Ros Schwartz.

"DO YOU KNOW THE LAND . . ."

1. Johann Wolfgang von Goethe, "Mignons Sehnsucht" ("Mignon's Longing"), in *Goethe: The Poet and the Age: Volume I: The Poetry of Desire (1749–1790)*, ed. Nicholas Boyle (Oxford: Oxford University Press, 1991).

A TREE PLANTED BY THE POET

1. Imre Kertész, *Fatelessness*, trans. Tim Wilkinson (New York: Vintage, 2004), 127.

THE FRUITS OF THE ELDERBERRY TREE

1. Bertolt Brecht, "Difficult Times," in *Bertolt Brecht: Poems, 1913–1956*, ed. John Willett and Ralph Manheim, trans. Michael Hamburger (New York: Methuen, 1979), 449. Used with permission from Taylor & Francis, Inc./Routledge, Inc.
2. *Gestus* is an acting technique developed by Brecht. It carries the sense of a combination of physical gestures and "gist," or attitude. It is a means by which "an attitude or single aspect of an attitude" is revealed, insofar as it is expressible in words or actions.

THE WEIGHT OF A WORD

1. This phrase is from Jan Skácel: *Der Dichter ist ein Radar unter den Linden* (The poet is a radar under the linden). Translated from the Czech into German by Reiner Kunze.

2. *Chemins fragiles*
   fragile
   est
   la terre au-dessus des sources : aucun arbre ne doit
   être *abattu, aucune racine*
   arrachée
   les sources pourraient
   tarir
   combien d'arbres sont
   abattus, combien de racines
   arrachées
   en nous

INTERIOR EXILE

1. Peter Huchel, "In the Frozen River," quoted in "Protest without an Echo," trans. Charlotte Collins. *Fikrun wa Fann,* Goethe-Institut, May 2008. http://www.goethe.de/ges/phi/prj/ffs/the/his/en3360550. htm.

THIS UNIVERSAL LANGUAGE

1. Yvonne Oddon, librarian at the Musée de l'Homme, was one of the three people who initially set up in June 1940 what was to become one of the most important Resistance networks, the Groupe du Musée de l'Homme.

TWO LINES FOR EACH LINE OF VERSE

1. The Service du Travail Obligatoire was the compulsory enlistment and deportation of hundreds of thousands of French workers to Nazi Germany to work as forced labor for the German war effort during World War II.
2. Tố Hữu, "Miền Nam," in *Trăm Bài Thơ* (Hanoi: Nhà Xuất Bản Văn Học, 1987).

FROM SHORE TO SHORE

1. Tố Hữu, "Mẹ Tôm," in *Trăm Bài Thơ* (Hanoi: Nhà Xuất Bản Văn Học, 1987).

2. Bertolt Brecht, "To Those Born Later," in *Bertolt Brecht: Poems, 1913–1956,* ed. John Willett and Ralph Manheim (New York: Methuen, 1979), 318.

BYWAYS

1. Mireille Gansel, "Le chant de l'homme," in *Des nouvelles de l'homme: visages du Vietnam: Hanoi 1972–1973* (Hanoi: Éditions Fleuve Rouge, 1985).
2. Tố Hữu, "Những người không chết," in *Từ ấy: thơ (1937–1946)* (Hanoi: Nhà Xuất Bản Văn Học, 1971).

NEW VERSION OF AN ANCIENT TALE

1. Chế Lan Viên, "Đối Thoại Mới Về Câu Chuyện Cổ," in *Tuyển Tập* (Hanoi: Édition Văn Học, 1985).
2. Chế Lan Viên, "Làm Hămlet ở Việt Nam," in *Tuyển Tập.*
3. "Petit frère sans plus attendre," in *Chants-poèmes des Monts et des Eaux: Anthologie des littératures orales des ethnies du Vietnam,* ed. Mireille Gansel (Paris: Sudestasie/UNESCO, 1986).

A SECOND GLASS OF LIGHT

1. René Char, "Comune Présence," in *René Char: The Myth and the Poem,* ed. James R. Lawler (Princeton, NJ: Princeton University Press, 1978).
2. René Char, "Leaves of Hypnos," in *Furor and Mystery and Other Writings,* trans. Mary Ann Caws and Nancy Kline (Boston: Black Widow Press, 2011).
3. René Char, "Tự Do," in *Đẹp hơn nước mắt,* trans. Tế Hanh (Hanoi: Édition Văn Học, 1983).

A SLIVER OF PLANE TREE BARK

1. Paul Celan, *Paul Celan and Nelly Sachs: Correspondence,* ed. Barbara Wiedemann, trans. Christopher Clark (New York: Sheep Meadow Press, 1995).

THE FOUR NOTEBOOKS

1. This expression was suggested to me by Alexandre Safran, in the section he wrote on teshuvah, "Le renouveau et la continuité," in his book *Lumières pour l'Avenir. Réflexions sur le Temps et l'Éternité,* Albin Michel, 2011. (Translator's note: Alexandre Safran (1910–2006) was chief rabbi in Romania during World War II and then chief rabbi in Geneva from 1948 for fifty years.)

2. Nelly Sachs, "O the Chimneys," in *"O the Chimneys": Selected Poems, Including the Verse Play "Eli,"* trans. Michael Hamburger (New York: Farrar, Straus & Giroux, 1967).

3. Nelly Sachs, *Paul Celan and Nelly Sachs: Correspondence,* ed. Barbara Wiedemann, trans. Christopher Clark (New York: Sheep Meadow Press, 1995).

4. Nelly Sachs, "O the Night of the Weeping Children!" in *Selected Poems.*

5. Nelly Sachs, "Someone Comes," in *Selected Poems.*

6. Nelly Sachs, "Ihr meine toten," in *Teile dich Nacht* (Berlin: Suhrkamp, 1971).

7. Esther Starobinski-Safran, "Quelques caractéristiques de la traduction de Buber et Rosenzweig Die Schrift," in *Rashi 1040–1990: hommage à Ephraïm E. Urbach ; Congrès européen des études juives,* ed. Gabrielle Sed-Rajna (Paris: Editions du Cerf, 1993), 777–87.

8. Nelly Sachs, "Time of Pupation," in *Selected Poems.*

9. Nelly Sachs, "Fleeing," in *Selected Poems.*

10. Nelly Sachs, "Stars Have Hearts and Mouths," in *The Seeker and Other Poems,* trans. Michael Hamburger and Ruth and Matthew Mead (New York: Farrar, Straus & Giroux, 1970).

11. Nelly Sachs, "The Candle That I Have Lit for You," trans. Sabine Smith and Laurence Sherr (Frankfurt: Suhrkamp Verlag, 1977).

12. Nelly Sachs, "Two Hands, Born to Give," in *The Seeker.*

13. Nelly Sachs, "Hands," in *Collected Poems, Nelly Sachs 1944–1949,* trans. Michael Hamburger, Ruth and Matthew Mead, and Michael Roloff (Los Angeles: Green Integer, 2011).

14. Nelly Sachs, "If the Prophets Broke In," trans. Catterel and Catherine Sommer, *Poems of Nelly Sachs in English: Beauty for Ashes* (blog), May 20, 2014, https://nellysachsenglish.wordpress.com/2014/05/20/if-the-prophets-broke-in/.

15. Nelly Sachs, "David," "Daniel," and "Sinai," in *The Seeker*.

16. Nelly Sachs, "The Seeker," in *The Seeker*.

17. Safran, *Lumières pour l'Avenir*.

18. The *Zohar* is a collection of commentaries on the *Torah*, the foundational work of Jewish mystical thought known as the Kabbalah.

19. Nelly Sachs, "Then Wrote the Scribe of *The Sohar*," in *Selected Poems*.

20. Ibid.

21. Nelly Sachs, "White in the Hospital Park," in *O Night, Divide,* trans. Andrew Shanks, 2015, http://www.nellysachs-translations.org.uk/teile.html#Krankenhauspark.

LANGUAGE OF CHILDHOOD

1. Nelly Sachs, "O the Night of the Weeping Children!" in *"O the Chimneys": Selected Poems, Including the Verse Play "Eli,"* trans. Michael Hamburger (New York: Farrar, Straus & Giroux, 1967).

2. Nelly Sachs, "Always," trans. Catterel and Catherine Sommer, *Poems of Nelly Sachs in English: Beauty for Ashes* (blog), May 20, 2014, https://nellysachsenglish.wordpress.com/2014/05/20/always/.

3. Imre Kertész, *Kaddish for an Unborn Child*, trans. Tim Wilkinson (New York: Vintage, 2004), 40–42.

The Feminist Press is a nonprofit educational organization founded to amplify feminist voices. FP publishes classic and new writing from around the world, creates cutting-edge programs, and elevates silenced and marginalized voices in order to support personal transformation and social justice for all people.

See our complete list of books at
feministpress.org